MAKE
Your
REQUEST
KNOWN

MAKE *Your* REQUEST KNOWN

Dr. Evette Hyder-Davis

Copyright © 2017 by Evette Hyder-Davis
All rights reserved.

No portion of this book may be reproduced, stored in a retrieval system, or transmitted in any form or by any means – electronic, mechanical, photocopy, recording, scanning, or other – except for brief quotations in reviews or articles, without the prior written permission of the publisher.

ISBN (13): 978-0-692-95631-1
ISBN/SKU: 9780692956311

All Scripture references in this journal are from the King James Version of the Bible, The Open Bible Edition. Copyright 1975 Thomas Nelson, Inc. Publishers.

Editing by Evette.Co
Cover Design by Evette.Co

Printed in the United States of America

Published by EVETTE.co
P.O. Box 34
Herndon, VA, USA 20172

Make Your Request Known

INTRODUCTION

Make Your Request Known, a journal for documenting your prayer request! Philippians 4:6 reads, "Be careful for nothing; but in every thing by prayer and supplication with thanksgiving let your requests be made known unto God." The Apostle Paul is suggesting to the church at Philippi that when prayers and petitions are made to God, it should be offered with thanksgiving and without worry. The key word for understanding that our prayers and petitions should be offered in faith is **careful**. The word **careful** in the Greek is **merimnaó** – meaning to be anxious and distracted. According to HELP word studies, **merimnaó** is an old verb for worry and anxiety that means to literally be divided and distracted. Therefore, the Apostle Paul is asking the church not to engage in distractions or to become divided.

How many Christians pray or petition God without worry and anxiety? It is usually worry and anxiety that warrants most Christians to pray. The purpose of this prayer journal is to document the prayers and petitions that you offer up to God and to keep track of the answers received.

I often have several petitions before God and I usually number them by importance of needing an answer. However, the number of petition God has answered (i.e. yes, no, or wait) cannot be numbered because I failed to document the request. Therefore, God has answered many prayers, which I have not documented and cannot refer to for encouragement.

Documenting your prayer or petition is very different from documenting received revelation. When God offers new revelation, I take out my journal and document what has been revealed. I include the date and time so that I am reminded when the revealed has manifested or come to pass.

I am new to documenting when God has answered my prayer or petition and I thought it would be great to take others on this journey of documenting answered prayer. It is important to remember the things God has promised, as well as, the prayers and petitions you have before Him. Christians can take pride in knowing that God cares about our prayers and petitions.

God gives you an answer whether favorable or unfavorable. However, it is an answer. Make Your Request Known has four components: (1) a passage of scripture for encouragement to the believer as you journal your prayers and petitions, (2) a yes or no check-in that will serve as an indicator of receiving God's answer, (3) two date

Make Your Request Known

stamps to record when you prayed and when God answered your prayer, and (4) a worry check-in to determine your level of worry and anxiety during your prayer time.

I hope this journal becomes a resource for all things God has done and will do in your life through answered prayer and petitions. May the Lord bless you and keep you is my prayer!

Dr. Evette Hyder-Davis

Make Your Request Known

"BUT MY GOD SHALL SUPPLY ALL YOUR NEED ACCORDING TO HIS RICHES IN GLORY BY CHRIST JESUS."
PHILIPPIANS 4:19 KJV

Journaling Date:

Answer Date:

God's Answer:
☐ Yes ☐ No

Worry and Anxiety:
☐ Yes ☐ No

Make Your Request Known

"THEREFORE I SAY UNTO YOU, WHAT THINGS SO EVER YE DESIRE, WHEN YE PRAY BELIEVE THAT YE RECEIVE THEM, AND YE SHALL HAVE THEM."
ST. MATTHEW 11:24 KJV

Journaling Date:

Answer Date:

God's Answer:
☐ Yes ☐ No

Worry and Anxiety:
☐ Yes ☐ No

Make Your Request Known

"NOT THAT WE ARE SUFFICIENT OF OURSELVES TO THINK ANY THING AS OF OURSELVES; BUT OUR SUFFICIENCY IS OF GOD."
II CORINTHIANS 3:5 KJV

Journaling Date:

Answer Date:

God's Answer:
☐ *Yes* ☐ *No*

Worry and Anxiety:
☐ *Yes* ☐ *No*

Make Your Request Known

"AND WHAT IS THE EXCEEDING GREATNESS OF HIS POWER TO US-WARD WHO BELIEVE, ACCORDING TO THE WORKING OF HIS MIGHTY POWER."
EPHESIANS 1:19 KJV

Journaling Date:

Answer Date:

God's Answer:
☐ *Yes* ☐ *No*

Worry and Anxiety:
☐ *Yes* ☐ *No*

Make Your Request Known

"I CAN DO ALL THINGS THROUGH CHRIST
WHICH STRENGTHENETH ME."
PHILIPPIANS 4:13 KJV

Journaling Date:

Answer Date:

God's Answer:
☐ Yes ☐ No

Worry and Anxiety:
☐ Yes ☐ No

Make Your Request Known

"NAY, IN ALL THESE THINGS WE ARE MORE THAN CONQUERORS THROUGH HIM THAT LOVED US."
ROMANS 8:37 KJV

Journaling Date:

Answer Date:

God's Answer:
☐ Yes ☐ No

Worry and Anxiety:
☐ Yes ☐ No

Make Your Request Known

"IF YE ABIDE IN ME AND MY WORDS ABIDE IN YOU, YE SHALL ASK WHAT YE WILL AND IT SHALL BE DONE UNTO YOU."
ST. JOHN 15:7 KJV

Journaling Date:

Answer Date:

God's Answer:
☐ Yes ☐ No

Worry and Anxiety:
☐ Yes ☐ No

Make Your Request Known

"BLESSED BE THE GOD AND FATHER OF OUR LORD JESUS CHRIST, WHO HATH BLESSED US WITH ALL SPIRITUAL BLESSINGS IN HEAVENLY PLACES IN CHRIST."
EPHESIANS 1:3 KJV

Journaling Date:

Answer Date:

God's Answer:
☐ *Yes* ☐ *No*

Worry and Anxiety:
☐ *Yes* ☐ *No*

Make Your Request Known

"AND WHATSOEVER YE SHALL ASK IN MY NAME, THAT WILL I DO THAT THE FATHER MAY BE GLORIFIED IN THE SON. IF YE SHALL ASK ANY THING IN MY NAME, I WILL DO IT."
ST. JOHN 14:13-14 KJV

Journaling Date:

Answer Date:

God's Answer:
☐ *Yes* ☐ *No*

Worry and Anxiety:
☐ *Yes* ☐ *No*

Make Your Request Known

"BLESS THE LORD, O MY SOUL, AND FORGET NOT ALL HIS BENEFITS: WHO FORGIVETH ALL THIN INIQUITIES; WHO HEALETH ALL THY DISEASE; WHO REDEEMETH THY LIFE FROM DESTRUCTION; WHO CROWNETH THEE WITH LOVING KINDNESS AND TENDER MERCIES; WHO SATISFIETH THY MOUTH WITH GOOD THINGS, SO THAT THY YOUTH IS RENEWED LIKE THE EAGLE'S."
PSALMS 103:2-5 KJV

Journaling Date:

Answer Date:

God's Answer:
☐ *Yes* ☐ *No*

Worry and Anxiety:
☐ *Yes* ☐ *No*

Make Your Request Known

"HE THAT SPARED NOT HIS OWN SON, BUT DELIVERED HIM UP FOR US ALL, HOW SHALL HE NOT WITH HIM ALSO FREELY GIVE US ALL THINGS?"
ROMANS 8:32 KJV

Journaling Date:

Answer Date:

God's Answer:
☐ Yes ☐ No

Worry and Anxiety:
☐ Yes ☐ No

Make Your Request Known

"AND ALL THINGS, WHATSOEVER YE SHALL ASK
IN PRAYER, BELIEVING, YE SHALL RECEIVE."
ST. MATTHEW 21:22 KJV

Journaling Date:

Answer Date:

God's Answer:
☐ *Yes* ☐ *No*

Worry and Anxiety:
☐ *Yes* ☐ *No*

Make Your Request Known

"AND HE SAID UNTO ME, MY GRACE IS SUFFICIENT FOR THEE: FOR MY STRENGTH IS MADE PERFECT IN WEAKNESS. MOST GLADLY THEREFORE WILL I RATHER GLORY IN MY INFIRMITIES, THAT THE POWER OF CHRIST MAY REST UPON ME."
II CORINTHIANS 12:9

Journaling Date:

Answer Date:

God's Answer:
☐ Yes ☐ No

Worry and Anxiety:
☐ Yes ☐ No

Make Your Request Known

ADDITIONAL NOTES

www.ingramcontent.com/pod-product-compliance
Lightning Source LLC
Chambersburg PA
CBHW072113290426
44110CB00014B/1899